Simple & Practical English

for Korean Students:
A Beginner's Course

Contents

About this book

This book is not for a one-sided lecture style class. It is based on active participation, pair work and simple conversation building. You get out what you put it.

이 책은 교수의 일방적인 수업이 아닌 학생의 참여가 주를 이루는 수업이다. "뿌린 대로 거둔다"라는 속담처럼 참여한 만큼 성취할 수 있을 것이다.

It's almost impossible to learn a language passively. If you are not actively participating, you will not improve.

여러분이 알다시피 언어는 능동적으로 배우는 것이기 때문에 적극적인 참여와 연습이 필요하다.

Personal Pronouns

These pronouns are very important in English.

Subject	Possessive (adj)	Object	Possessive
I	My	Me	Mine
You	Your	You	Yours
He	His	Him	His
She	Her	Her	Hers
We	Our	Us	Ours
They	Their	Them	Theirs

The same thing can be said in different ways depending on the pronoun used.

 I am from Seoul.
My hometown is Seoul.

This is my pen.
This pen is mine.

She is from Seoul.
Her hometown is Seoul.

This is her pen.
This pen is hers.

100 most Common English Verbs

1. Add	추가하다	19. Create	만들다	37. Include	포함하다
2. Allow	허용하다	20. Cut	자르다	38. Keep	유지하다
3. Appear	나타나다	21. Die	죽다	39. Kill	죽이다
4. Ask	묻다	22. Do	하다	40. Know	알다
5. Be	이다/되다	23. Expect	기대하다	41. Lead	끌다
6. Become	-이 되다	24. Fall	떨어지다	42. Learn	배우다
7. Believe	믿다	25. Feel	느끼다	43. Leave	떠나다
8. Begin	시작하다	26. Find	찾다	44. Let	허락하다
9. Bring	가져오다	27. Follow	따르다	45. Like	좋아하다
10. Build	짓다	28. Get	받다	46. Live	살다
11. Buy	사다	29. Give	주다	47. Look	보다
12. Call	전화하다	30. Go	가다	48. Lose	잃다
13. Can	-할 수 있다	31. Grow	자라다	49. Love	사랑하다
14. Change	바꾸다	32. Happen	일어나다	50. Make	만들다
15. Come	오다	33. Have	가지다	51. May	-할 수 있다
16. Consider	고려하다	34. Hear	듣다	52. Mean	뜻을 두다
17. Continue	계속하다	35. Help	돕다	53. Meet	만나다
18. Could	-할 수 있었다	36. Hold	쥐다	54. Might	-할 것 같다

55. Move	움직이다					
56. Must	해야 하다	**71.** Seem	-인 것 같다	**86.** Tell	말하다
57. Need	필요하다	**72.** Send	보내다	**87.** Think	생각하다
58. Open	열다	**73.** Serve	제공하다	**88.** Turn	회전하다
59. Offer	권하다	**74.** Set	놓다	**89.** Try	노력하다
60. Pay	지불하다	**75.** Should	해야 한다	**90.** Understand	이해하다
61. Play	놀다	**76.** Show	보여 주다	**91.** Use	사용하다
62. Provide	제공하다	**77.** Sit	앉다	**92.** Wait	기다
63. Put	놓다	**78.** Speak	말하다	**93.** Walk	걷다
64. Reach	도달하다	**79.** Spend	보내다	**94.** Want	원하다
65. Read	읽다	**80.** Stand	서다	**95.** Watch	보다
66. Remain	남아 있다	**81.** Start	시작하다	**96.** Will	-할 것이다
67. Remember	기억하다	**82.** Stay	머무르다	**97.** Win	이기다
68. Run	달리다	**83.** Stop	멈추다	**98.** Work	일하다
69. Say	말하다	**84.** Take	가져가다	**99.** Would	-일 것이다
70. See	보다	**85.** Talk	말하다	**100.** Write	쓰다

Simple & Practical English for Korean Students: A Beginner's Course

Unit 1

Simple Present Tense

be verbs

Simple Present Tense
be verbs

The general pattern is

subject + verb + object

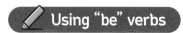 Using "be" verbs

Be verbs = am, is, are

 e.g.

I am a university student.

He is a university student.

We are university students.

 Questions

• Yes/No questions

Are you from Korea?
Yes, I am.
No, I'm not.

Is today Monday?
Yes, it is.
No, it's not.

• Information questions

Where are you from?
I'm from ……．

What day is it today?
Today is ……．

See the appendix **page 94** for rules on contractions.

 Using action verbs

Do, does

 I do homework every day.
He does homework every day.
We do homework every day.

Do, does can be replaced with any verb.

 I play badminton on Monday.
He eats pizza for dinner.
We study English at school.

 Questions

In the question form, the action verb is added to "do, does".

•Yes/No questions

Do you eat pizza?
    Yes, I do.
    No, I don't.

Does your friend play badminton?
    Yes, she does.
    No, she doesn't.

•Information questions

What do you study?
    I study English.

Where does your friend study?
    He studies at university.

 **Practice**

Fill in the blanks to make the questions. Some are "yes/no" questions, some are information questions. Some are "be" verbs, some are action verbs.

● 주요표현 연습(Pattern Drill)

1. _____ your name?

2. _____ your teacher from Canada?

3. _____ you from?

4. _____ you do after school?

5. _____ your birthday?

6. _____ they from Australia?

7. _____ their favorite sport?

8. _____ your friend do in the weekends?

9. _____ you like your school?

10. _____ you do in your free time?

● Present Tense and 3rd Person Singular

- Present tense 1st person
  I have a gold watch.
  I sketch people.

- Present tense 2nd person
  You have a gold watch.
  You sketch people.

- Present tense 3rd person
  Tom has a gold watch.
  Tina sketches people.

Fill in the blank with the correct form of the present tense verb.

My cousin _____(be) an art major. She _____(sketch) people very well. When she _____(go) to the park, she _____(find) interesting things to sketch. She _____(say) people doing something together _____(be) the best thing to sketch because she _____(put) feeling into the drawing. Sometimes she _____(draw) children playing, or families sitting together. Her friend really _____(like) her drawings, as well as other people, so my cousin _____(give) her drawings to friends. Sometimes people can see her drawings in cafes or offices. The drawings _____(be) great!

🔍 Questions from the story

1. What's her hobby?

2. Where does she like to go?

3. What does she try to find?

4. Who likes her drawings?

5. Where can people see her drawings?

6. What does she say is the best thing to sketch?

7. Why does she think so?

Answer the questions. Then ask your classmates. Use "he" or "she", when you write their answers. Don't just copy, listen to the answers. Try to use only English.

1. What's your name?

You:

Classmate:

2. Where is your hometown?

You:

Classmate:

3. When is your birthday?

You:

Classmate:

4. What's your favorite food?

You:

Classmate:

5. What kind of music do you like?

You:

Classmate:

6. What sport do you like?

You:

Classmate:

7. What do you do in your free time?

You:

Classmate:

8. What's something you don't like?

You:

Classmate:

9. What is your dream vacation?

You:

Classmate:

10. What color are your shoes?

You:

Classmate:

Simple & Practical
English for
Korean Students: A
Beginner's Course

Simple & Practical English for Korean Students: A Beginner's Course

Unit 2

Simple Present Tense

action verbs

Simple Present Tense
action verbs

 Using action verbs

Action Verbs = go, do, meet etc.

e.g. I go to the park to exercise.

He does yoga every day.

We meet every Friday.

 Questions

• Yes/No questions

Do you play baseball?
  Yes, I do.
  No, I don't.

Does she like pizza?
  Yes, she does.
  No, she doesn't.

• Information questions

Where do you hang out?
  I hang out at⋯.

What do you eat at the department store?
  I eat⋯.

Fill in the verbs to make the story. The following verbs are used twice. Sometimes the negative forms "don't" and "doesn't" can be used.

| Watch   Work   Study   Live   Is   Have   Like   are |

My name _____ Jenny. My friend, Kim, _____ in my class at school. We _____ both students. We _____ different in a lot of ways. I _____ 3 brothers but Kim _____ any brothers or sisters. I _____ with my parents. Kim _____ alone. At University I _____ design and Kim _____ science. Kim doesn't _____ , but I _____ at a restaurant. I _____ rock music, but Kim _____ it. She _____ YouTube videos. We usually _____ movies together on Saturdays.

🗨️✓ **Questions from the story**

1. Where does Jenny work?

2. What is Kim's hobby?

3. Who lives alone?

4. Is Jenny an only child?

5. What does Kim study?

6. What do they usually do on Saturdays?

This is a simple speaking exercise. Ask simple present tense questions of your classmates to see what you have in common.

 A: "What is your favorite nut?"
B: "I like peanuts."
A: "Me too."

It can be done in the negative also.

 A: "What's a food that you don't like?"
B: "I don't like pumpkin soup."
A: "I don't either."

Work with a partner and try to find 1 or 2 things that you both like, and both don't like.

Find 3 different people in your class that have common likes and dislikes with you. Make a note and share once the exercise is over.

Present Tense Common Mistakes

A common mistake often made in present tense is not attaching an "-s" on the verb if the subject is he, she, or it.

 X She <u>go</u> to school in the morning.

O She <u>goes</u> to school in the morning.

This is a small mistake, but it is important for using the present tense correctly. He, she, or it can also take the form of names and other nouns.

 (he) Tom eats pizza/ (she) My friend, Mina likes comics.

(it) The car goes fast.

If the sentence is negative, the "do" takes the "-s".

 Sylvester <u>does</u> not drive a car.

Another common mistake is to use the "be" verb together with an action verb.

 X We are go to the store.   O We go to the store.

Correct the mistakes following the information above

1. Her brother not study every day.

_____ .

2. They are study at night.

_____ .

3. I goes to Busan in summer.

_____ .

Simple & Practical English for Korean Students: A Beginner's Course

Present Continuous Tense

verb + ing

Unit 3

Present Continuous Tense
verb + ing

To show that an action is continuing over a period of time, add "ing" to the verb.

When using the "ing" form, a "be" verb am, is, are must also be used.

 He is wearing a white hat.   (unit 2: He wears a white hat.)

• Positive

I am eating chicken.

She is wearing blue jeans.

They are studying English.

• Negative

I am not eating chicken.

She isn't wearing blue jeans.

They aren't studying English.

💬 Make the sentences using the "be + ing" form.

1. Karen is at the market. She _____ food. (buy)

2. My friend and I _____ dinner now. (eat)

3. She _____ the bus to school now. (ride)

4. He _____ right now. (study/not) He _____ on his phone. (play)

5. You _____ badminton now (play/not). You _____ English. (tudy)

6. Tom and Lucy are at the library. They _____ homework. (do)

7. I _____ to school (walk) because it _____ . (rain/not)

8. Today is very hot. We _____ water. (drink)

9. It's Saturday. I _____ (relax) and _____ a book. (read)

10. We are hungry. We _____ chicken delivery. (order)

💬 Make the sentences about people right now.

1. The teacher _____ .

2. I _____ .

3. My friend _____ .

4. My mother/father _____ .

• Yes/No

Is she studying?
Yes she is./No she isn't.

Are you going to school?
Yes I am./No I'm not.

• Information

Who is she talking to?
She is talking to her mother.

Where are you going?
I'm going to school.

Look at the answers, make the questions.

1. A: _____ ?

   B: I'm buying some juice.

2. A: _____ ?

   B: We're going to a concert.

3. A: _____ ?

   B: The restaurant is closing at 11pm.

4. A: _____ ?

   B: The movie is starting at 3pm.

5. A: _____ ?

   B: They are listening to rock music.

6. A: _____ ?

   B: They are going there by bus.

Add these verbs into the following dialogue. Use the present continuous tense.

| Watch(보다) | Play(놀다) | Do(하다) | Wear(입다) |

💬 On the phone

Mark	Hey Ron!
Ron	Oh, hi Mark!
Mark	What are you doing right now?
Ron	I'm ❶ _____ cat videos on youtube. They're so funny.
Mark	Ha! I'm ❷ _____ with my cat now. Maybe I can make a video.
Ron	Want to do something? I am bored. I'm just sitting around watching videos.
Mark	Yea, I'm not ❸ _____ anything.
Ron	Let's meet at Sadang Station.
Mark	Ok, but how will I find you? What are you wearing?
Ron	I'm ❹ _____ a black hat and white sweater. You?
Mark	I'm ❺ _____ my new long padded jacket. You'll know when you see it.
Ron	Cool! See you soon.

✅ Questions

1. What is Ron doing?

2. What is Mark doing?

3. What is Ron wearing?

4. What is Mark Wearing?

Clothing is also a continuous situation.

e.g. What are you wearing?
What is your friend wearing?
I'm wearing jeans and a shirt.
He is wearing a T-shirt and a hat.

Speaking practice

With a partner, Choose 3 people below. Your partner chooses the other 3. Draw clothes on the 3 people you have chosen. Your partner will ask you questions about what they are wearing. Describe the clothes you have drawn and your partner will try to draw only from your description.

No looking!

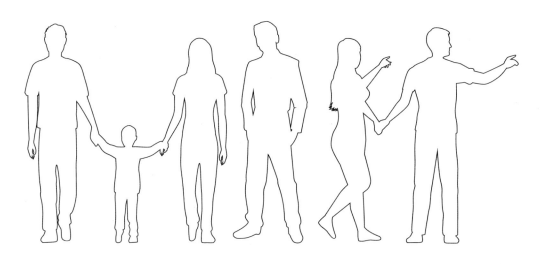

| Sam | Mike | Sarah | Brad | Jane | Tom |

Present Continuous Common Mistakes.

Common mistakes using the present continuous is confusing which form of "be" to use in agreement with the subject.

 e.g. X   We is eating kimbab now.

O   We <u>are</u> eating kimbab now.

Or it is possible to forget the "be" verb.

 e.g. X   We going to Lotte World.

O   We <u>are</u> going to Lotte World.

Another mistake that comes up often is using words to describe time that don't agree with the "right now" of present continuous.

 e.g. X   I am eating kimbab sometimes.

O   I eat kimbab sometimes. (must be simple present)

 Correct the mistakes following the information above.

1. I running in the park right now.

_____.

2. They is meeting in front of Anyang Station.

_____.

3. I am watching Youtube videos always.

_____.

Simple & Practical English for Korean Students: A Beginner's Course

Unit 4

Simple Future Tense

Will, be going to

Simple Future Tense
Will, be going to

The general pattern is

subject + verb + object

Be verbs am, is, are now become

"will, be going to"

 e.g. He <u>will</u> be a university student next year.

We <u>are going to</u> be university students next year.

 Questions

• Yes/No questions

Will you eat pizza for lunch?
 Yes, I will.
 No, I will not/won't.

Is it going to rain tomorrow?
 Yes, it is.
 No, it isn't.

• Information questions

What will you eat?
 I will eat ....
 I won't eat ....

What are you going to do tomorrow?
 I'm going to ....
 I'm not going to ....

Fill in the blanks. Use "will/won't".

1. Put on a jacket. It _____ be cold today.

2. I know your birthday is this Friday. I _____ forget.

3. I'm hungry. I _____ go the convenience store now.

4. I hate studying. I _____ do homework after school today.

5. It's Friday today. I _____ eat chicken with friends.

Now use "be going to/be not going to".
- For planned actions or things that are sure to happen.

1. I _____ graduate at the end of next year.

2. We _____ go to the party. We must study for a test.

3. My friend _____ travel to Japan this vacation.

4. He _____ save money. He wants to buy a car.

5. You _____ learn a lot in this class.

💬 Answer the following questions about the future.

1. What will you do tonight?

   _____.

2. What are you going to do this weekend?

   _____.

3. What will you do this vacation?

   _____.

4. What are you going to do in 5 years?

   _____.

5. What will you do in 10 years?

   _____.

💬 Now things that you will NOT do.

1. What will you not do tonight?

   _____.

2. What aren't you going to do this weekend?

   _____.

3. What will you not do this vacation?

   _____.

4. What aren't you going to do in 5 years?

   _____.

5. What will you not do in 10 years?

   _____.

Answer the questions, then ask classmates. Ask each question to a different classmate. Remember to use "he" and "she" when you write their answers.

1. What's something you will buy in the future?

   You:

   Classmate:

2. Where are you maybe going to live in the future?

   You:

   Classmate:

3. Are you going to travel, or visit, somewhere in the future? Where?

   You:

   Classmate:

4. What's your dream?

   You:

   Classmate:

5. What is something that you will learn, or start?

   You:

   Classmate:

6. What is something you are going to do with a group of friends?

   You:

   Classmate:

7. Will you marry in the future? When?

   You:

   Classmate:

8. What is something dangerous, or unusual, that you want to do?

   You:

   Classmate:

When using the future tense "will," it is a helping verb so the main verb must be in base form. This means any change to the verb will be incorrect.

 X   I will doing my homework.

X   Mark will studies English.

O   I will <u>go</u> home.

When using "be going to" remember that this phrase works as a helping verb so a main verb is also needed to complete the sentence.

 X   He is going to games.

O   He is going to <u>play</u> games.

When the main verb is "go" the sentence looks correct, but it is not considered future tense. Be sure to have a main verb when using "be going to" in a sentence.

 X   He is going to Japan. (present continuous, not future tense)

O   He is going to <u>go</u> to Japan.

💬 Correct the sentences using the information above.

1. Luna is going to Malaysia.

   _____ .

2. His friend will buying a new car.

   _____ .

3. I am going to eating pizza for dinner tonight.

   _____ .

Simple & Practical English for Korean Students: A Beginner's Course

Unit

5

Simple Past Tense

Regular, irregular verbs

Unit 5

Simple Past Tense
Regular, irregular verbs

The general pattern is

subject + past tense verb + object

 I played badminton yesterday.

She walked to school last week.

They ate cold noodles in Busan last summer.∗

∗ Many past verbs in English are irregular.

 **Regular verbs**

Regular verbs are simple and have "ed" at the end.

 Play → Play<u>ed</u>

Listen → Listen<u>ed</u>

Study → Stud<u>ied</u>

 **IrRegular verbs**

Irregular verbs do not have "ed".

 e.g. Do → Did   Buy → Bought   Drink → Drank

Be → Was, Were	Buy → Bought	Meet → Met
Bring → Brought	Get → Got	Feel → Felt
Catch → Caught	Give → Gave	Say → Said
Come → Came	Go → Went	Take → Took
Eat → Ate	Know → Knew	Tell → Told
Fall → Fell	Leave → Left	Think → Thought
Find → Found	Make → Made	Swim → Swam

Questions

• Yes/No questions

Did you eat pizza for breakfast?
   Yes, I did.
   No, I did not/didn't.

Did it rain yesterday?
   Yes, it did.
   No, it didn't.

• Information questions

What did you eat for dinner last night?
   I ate ....
   I didn't eat ....

What did you do last weekend?
   I met my friends.
   I did not do my homework.

The important thing to note here is that when asking a question in simple past tense, The only marker used is "did". The present tense of the action verb is always used.

We do **not** say "Did you ate breakfast?" There is no need to add the past tense of "eat" because the question begins with the past tense "did".

Only when making a statement do we use the past tense of the action verb. "I **ate** breakfast at 7am." Only a single past tense marker is needed.

Practice writing verbs in past tense by writing the correct form into the story.

Last Summer, I _____ (go) to Busan. I _____ (take) the fast train to Busan Station. It _____ (be) so fast! I _____ (go) to Haeundae Beach first. I _____ (swim) in the water and _____ (drink) some soda while relaxing. It _____ (be) so nice. Later, I _____ (go) to the night market and _____ (buy) some street food. The night market _____ (have) a good atmosphere. I also _____ (try) really delicious seafood. After, I _____ (go) to Gwangali Beach and _____ (take) pictures next to the water. The ocean wind _____ (feel) really nice. I want to go to Busan again.

💬 Write the correct past action and then check true or false.

1. I _____ BBQ with friends last week. (eat)

2. I _____ the new drama on MBC yesterday. (see)

3. I _____ my friend to see what was happening. (text)

4. I _____ breakfast this morning. (have)

5. I _____ late playing games on my phone last night. (stay up)

6. I _____ all of my money on payday. (spend)

7. I _____ a lot of water last summer. (drink)

💬 Rewrite the above 7 sentences into yes/no questions and then ask your partner and check true of false based on their answer.

Yes/No Questions	Yes	No
1.		
2.		
3.		
4.		
5.		
6.		
7.		

💬 Discuss these questions with a partner and share the answer with the class.

1. What is something you bought recently? Was it expensive?

2. Where did you live when you were young?

3. Where did you visit in the past? Was it fun?

4. What was your dream when you were a child?

5. What is something interesting that you learned?

6. What did you do with your friends the last time you met them?

7. What is something unusual or dangerous that you have done?

✏️ Finish the stories

Use sequence vocabulary to add to the story. Here is an example:

• I went to the park.

• I saw my friend there.

• My friend had a dog with him.

• Then we played with the dog all day.

• After that we ate fried chicken.

 Finish the stories below with what happened next.

1. • Mike met Sarah at the café.

   • He and Sarah go to the same university.

   • Sarah told Mike _____ .

   • Then _____ .

   • After that _____ .

   • _____ .

2. • Stuart was in an old hotel.

   • He opened the door of his room and saw

   _____ .

   • Next _____ .

   • After that _____ .

   • _____ .

💬 Review of tenses, Present, Future and Past.

Choose an appropriate verb for each sentence and write it in the correct past tense form. Then change to present, future and present continuous tense.

Fall(떨어지다)	Go(가다)	Eat(먹다)	Give(주다)	Play(놀다)
Find(찾다)	Get up(일어나다)	Come(오다)	Take(가져가다)	Catch(걸리다)
Be(되다)	Pay(지불하다)	Bring(가져오다)	Meet(만나다)	Travel(여행하다)

Present: Dr Lee _____ early in the morning for his class.

　　Present Continuous: _____.

　　Future (going to): _____.

　　Past: _____.

Present: My friend _____ a cake to the class and we _____ it with everybody.

　　Present Continuous: _____.

　　Future (going to): _____.

　　Past: _____.

Present: My dad _____ to Canada during the winter and _____ a cold there.

　　Present Continuous: _____.

　　Future (going to): _____.

　　Past: _____.

Present: I _____ to New York city because my family lives there.

　　Present Continuous: _____.

　　Future (going to): _____.

　　Past: _____.

1. Present: They _____ basketball on Saturday in a team.

   Present Continuous: _____.

   Future (going to): _____.

   Past: _____.

2. Present: She _____ him on the airplane to Japan and _____

   in love with him.

   Present Continuous: _____.

   Future (going to): _____.

   Past: _____.

3. Present: Chris _____ his girlfriend a nice birthday present.

   So she _____ for the dinner.

   Present Continuous: _____.

   Future (going to): _____.

   Past: _____.

4. Present: I _____ someone's wallet on the street. I _____ it

   to the police station.

   Present Continuous: _____.

   Future (going to): _____.

   Past: _____.

5. Present: My mother _____ home really late from work.

   Present Continuous: _____.

   Future (going to): _____.

   Past: _____.

Simple & Practical English for Korean Students: A Beginner's Course

Unit 6

Gerunds and Infinitives

to + verb, verb + ing

Unit 6

Gerunds and Infinitives

to + verb, verb + ing

A gerund is a noun made from a verb by adding "ing"

 I <u>like eating</u> **pizza.** (Unit 2: I <u>like</u> pizza. Unit 3: I <u>am eating</u> pizza.)

Gerunds are often used to link feelings with actions and objects.

Main verbs can include feelings, past actions and preferences.

Main verb	Gerund verb	Object
Like	Eat	Pizza
Don't like	Drink	Cola
Enjoy	Drive	Cars
Love	Play	Basketball
Hate	Watch	Movies
Remember	Ride	A bicycle
Try/Tried	Cook	Noodles
Start/Started	Wear	Sunglasses

Make Gerund sentences using the above main verbs, gerund verbs and objects.

1. _____.

2. _____.

3. _____.

4. _____ .

5. _____ .

6. _____ .

An infinitive is the "to" form of the verb.

 I like <u>to eat</u> pizza.   The "ing" form is not used here.

Main verbs can include feelings, past actions and preferences.

Main verb	Infinitive verb	Object
Like	Eat	Lobster
Don't like	Drink	Champagne
Love	Drive	A BMW
Hate	Travel	Europe
Want	See	A live concert
Don't want	Ride	A horse
Promise	Study	English
Hope	Get	A great job

Make Infinitive sentences using the above main verbs, infinitive verbs and objects.

1. _____ .

2. _____ .

3. _____ .

4. _____ .

5. _____ .

6. _____ .

A timeframe can also be added.

> **e.g.**   I like to read books <u>on the weekend.</u>
> He doesn't like to study <u>in summer vacation.</u>
>
> I like reading books <u>on the weekend.</u>
> He doesn't like studying <u>in summer vacation.</u>

Make your own sentences using either form. Add in a timeframe where needed.

1. I want to _____ .

2. I love to _____ .

3. I enjo _____ .

4. I lik _____ .

5. I don't like _____ .

6. I hope to _____ .

7. I promise to _____ .

8. I try to _____ .

9. I like to _____ .

Group practice

- What are you into? What are you not into?
- Work together in a small group. Tell each other what you are into, and why?

 Questions to think about

- What do you like?
- Why?
- When did you start to like it?
- Do other people like it too?

- What don't you like?
- Why not?
- When did you start to dislike it?
- Why/why not?

 Gerunds and Infinitives

Gerunds and infinitives are nouns that look like verbs.

Gerund	Infinitive
• Meet (verb) → Meeting (noun) • Drink (verb) → Drinking (noun)	• Meet (verb) → to meet (noun) • Drink (verb) → to drink (noun)

• The general pattern is:
   subject + verb + gerund + object
 	
 I like to eating cereal for breakfast.
   I enjoy* talking with my friends.
	• The general pattern is:
	   subject + verb + infinitive + object
	
	 I hope** to play games tomorrow.
	   I want** to travel to Europe.

* enjoy must be used with gerunds only.

** hope and want must be used with infinitives only.

It is possible to explain two actions in one simple sentence using gerunds and infinitives.

I like pizza + I eat pizza

↓

I like eating pizza

✎ **Gerunds and Infinitives Common Mistakes**

It is possible for there to be some confusion between when to use a gerund and when to use an infinitive. Because of this, using the gerund "-ing" with the infinitive "to" can happen.

   X I remember to going on a trip.

   O I remember going on a trip.

There are some verbs that can't be used with gerunds. There is no rule for which words can't be used so they have to be memorized. The common verbs "hope" and "want" can't be used with gerunds.

   X I hope going to Busan.

   X I want eating pizza.

There are some verbs that can't be used with infinitives. There is no rule for which words can't be used so they have to be memorized. The common verbs "enjoy" and "dislike" can't be used with infinitives.

   X I enjoy to drive my car.

   X I dislike to go to the market.

💬 Correct the sentences following the information above.

1. I want going home.

   _____.

2. I like to taking a trip to Busan.

   _____.

3. I enjoy to watch videos online.

   _____.

Simple & Practical English for Korean Students: A Beginner's Course

Unit

7

Locations and Directions

Where, how to get to ⋯

Unit 7

Locations and Directions

Where, how to get to …

Use locations to tell where something is. Locations do not move.

Above	Under	In	On	Next to	Between
Where is the clock?	Where are the people?	Where are your pencils?	Where are your crayons?	Where is your coffee?	Where is the notepad?
It is above the plant.	They're under the bridge.	They are in the cup.	They're on the table.	It is next to the computer.	It's between his hands.

Look at the picture and complete the sentences.

1. The desks are _____ the classroom.

2. The clock is _____ the blackboard.

3. The paper is _____ the desk.

4. The cup is _____ the teacher's desk.

Fill in the blanks in the story using the following location words.

| Next to | on | above | in | under | between |

I am always in my room. I don't clean it often, but I know where everything is. I will tell you where my most important items are. I have a nice gaming PC ❶ _____ my bed. I play games there every night with friends. I have a heating mat ❷ _____ my bed to keep me warm on cold nights. I have a projector so I can watch movies on the ceiling ❸ _____ my bed. I have a pet turtle ❹ _____ a glass case. His name is Bitey. He is always ❺ _____ the water. I always have my guitar ❻ _____ my bed and my desk. I play it sometimes. I love my room!

Questions

1. Where is Fredrick's gaming PC?

2. Where is Fredrick's heating mat?

3. Where is Bitey?

4. Where is Fredrick's guitar?

Things around your area:

Can you answer these simple questions about the locations of things in and around your area?

- Where is the closest ATM?

- Where is the closest Bookstore?

- Where is a delicious chicken restaurant?

- Where is the bus stop?

- Where is the train station?

Use directions to tell **how to go** somewhere. Directions show movement.

Go straight	Turn left	Turn right

These are 3 simple directions, but can be added to:
- Go up/down the stairs or elevator
- Go in/out of the room or building
- Go across the street

Also "go" can be changed into any other word for movement.

 Walk, ride, drive etc.

 **Make a map of your dream neighborhood.**

- Map Rules: 6+ buildings (1 house)

                       4+ streets

You can add anything into your neighborhood:

- Bank, restaurant, bakery, park, bus stop, candy store etc.

Work with a partner to give directions from place to place on your map. Then do the same thing with your partner's map.

Now give directions to the following places. Finish with giving a location.

• How do I get to the closest ATM?

• How do I get to the closest bookstore?

• How do I get to the nearest chicken restaurant?

• How do I get to the bus stop?

• How do I get to the train station?

It is useful to think of locations as "where" and directions as "how to go" when practicing these concepts.

 Where is the keyboard? ⟶ Under the computer screen.

How do I go/get to Lottle ⟶ Go straight, pass Lotte World
World?   Mall, and turn right.

Directions are given in Imperative sentences so a subject is not needed.

 X You go straight.   O Go straight.

Some location words can be phrases more than one word. Make sure to use the whole phrase

 X It is next the car.   O It is next to the car.

Correct the sentences using the information above.

1. Go straight and on the left.

   _____.

2. You turn left and you pass the bank.

   _____.

3. I am standing next the building.

   _____.

Simple & Practical English for Korean Students: A Beginner's Course

Unit
8

Can/Can't for
Ability and Rules

Can, Can't

Unit 8

Can/Can't for Ability and Rules

Can, Can't

Can and Can't are used for ability.

> **Ex.** I can play basketball, but I can't swim.
> He can speak Korean, but he can't speak Japanese.

"Could/Couldn't" are used in the past tense.

> **Ex.** When I was a baby, I couldn't walk.
> When I was young, I could sing well.

Answer these questions for ability:

- What is something that you can do?

- What is something that you can't do?

- What can you do now, that you couldn't do 10 years ago?

💬 They can also be used to show something is allowed or to state rules.

Ex. I'm over 18, so I can drink alcohol.

don't have a driver's license, so I can't drive on the road.

💬 "Could/Couldn't" are used in the past tense.

Ex. When I was in middle school, I couldn't drink beer.

When I turned 18, I could get a driver's license.

💬 Answer these questions for permission:

• What is something that you can do?

• What is something that you can't do?

• What is something that you can't do now, that you could do 10 years ago?

💬 Rules for your classroom. Work with a partner, make a list of 10 rules, or advice, for your major subject(주요 과목). 5 positive, 5 negative. Do you agree with them? Why?

Positive	Negative
1.	1.
2.	2.
3.	3.
4.	4.
5.	5.

Situations. Work with a partner to decide what you can do in the following situations.

1. You and a friend are going to a party. It's raining and the traffic is very heavy. Your friend wants to drive. What can you do and why?

2. You and a friend plan to go the river for a picnic on Saturday. The weather forecast is for rain. What can you do and why?

3. You and a friend are at the beach. It's hot and very sunny. Your friend wants to go swimming. What can you do and why?

4. You have exams next week. Your friends want to eat chicken and drink beer. What can you do and why?

Simple & Practical English for Korean Students: A Beginner's Course

Count and
Non-Count Nouns

Plural nouns

Unit 9

Count and Non-Count Nouns
Plural nouns

 Some nouns in English can be counted (가산 명사).

> e.g. Tom has <u>5 tomatoes.</u>
>
> I bought <u>2</u> new <u>cellphones.</u>
>
> My uncle has a farm with <u>25 chickens.</u>

 Some nouns can't be counted because of their type (불가산 명사).

> e.g. Tom has a lot of <u>rice.</u>
>
> I bought some <u>water.</u>
>
> My uncle has a lot of <u>money.</u>

 If the food is too small to count, a main dish, or a liquid(액체)**, it isn't counted.**

> e.g. I put <u>sugar</u> into the cooking mix. (too small to count)
>
> I ate a lot of <u>chicken</u> at the restaurant. (main dish)
>
> I have some <u>water</u> in the refrigerator. (liquid)

I have chicken.

I have a chicken.

I have chickens.

💬 **Practice putting the food into the correct category.**

milk	tomato	chicken	ramen	potato
coffee	banana	oil	pork	pepper paste
rice	onion	toast	egg	bacon
apple	kimchi	butter		

Count foods   Non-Count foods

💬 Some very common nouns can take both forms.

> **Ex.** I would like a <u>coffee</u> please. `Uncountable.`
> I would like 2 <u>coffees</u> please. `Countable.`

In the first sentence, coffee is uncountable, as it should be. In the second sentence, it is countable, but this is because the words "cups of" have not been said. For the sentence to be fully correct it should be:

> **Ex.** I would like 2 <u>cups</u> of coffee please. `Countable.`

💬 Substances are usually uncountable nouns:

- Do you want some <u>cake</u>?
- <u>Coffee</u> before bed makes it hard to sleep.
- Too much <u>beer</u> makes me sleepy.

💬 but they can also be used as countable nouns:

- I will order a wine, please. = I will order a (glass of) wine.
- They sell a lot of beer. = They sell a lot of (different <u>kinds</u> of) beer.
- They had more than 25 beers. = They had over 25 (kinds of) beer.
- This wine is delicious. = This (bottle of) wine is delicious.

Even though it may not be totally correct, it is so commonly used among English speakers that the countable nouns can be left out.

Try to work out if the underlined noun is countable or uncountable:

1. Do you want some <u>tea</u> or coffee?

Countable.
Uncountable.

2. Please give us two <u>beers</u>.

Countable.
Uncountable.

3. Do you like <u>sugar</u> in your coffee?

Countable.
Uncountable.

4. Yes, one <u>sugar</u>, please.

Countable.
Uncountable.

5. For this cake, you'll need 400g of <u>flour</u>.

Countable.
Uncountable.

6. You spilled some <u>food</u> on your shirt.

Countable.
Uncountable.

7. Can I have some <u>cheese</u>, please?

Countable.
Uncountable.

8. Can I have a <u>cookie</u>, please?

Countable.
Uncountable.

9. Please eat the last <u>chocolate</u> in the box.

Countable.
Uncountable.

10. Can you buy me a bar of <u>chocolate</u>?

Countable.
Uncountable.

Using **a/an/some** for count nouns and some for non-count. ("some" is used for an unspecified amount)

e.g. I ate <u>a</u> strawberry.   I ate <u>an</u> orange.

I ate chicken.   I ate <u>some</u> strawberries.

I ate some oranges.   I ate <u>some</u> chicken.

Write "a/an" or "some" in the blank.

1. I am going to meet _____ friends at 6pm.

2. We have _____ homework today.

3. I have _____ picture from our trip.

4. She is cooking _____ spaghetti tonight.

5. We ordered _____ bottle of cola.

6. He put in _____ spicy sauce to give the rice more flavor.

7. Virgil bought _____ fresh kimchi at the market.

8. We are cooking _____ apple pie for tonight's event.

9. I need to cu _____ big watermelon.

10. Stella and her friends ate _____ ice-cream cake.

💬 We can be specific(특정), or non-specific(비특정) when using these kinds of nouns.

Specific for countable nouns	Non-specific or for non-countable
• There is a pen. = There is one pen. • There are 20 students.	• There are some pens. • There are a lot of students. • There is some milk. • There is a little juice.

• To be specific, use the number of items. 1, 2, 3 etc.

• To be general for countable nouns use "a few".

• To be general for non-countable nouns use "a little".

• "Some" and "a lot of" can be used for both countable and non-countable nouns.

• Be specific or be general. Now talk with your partner, what can you make using the Things in your refrigerators?

💬 Please My Refrigerator!
List 8 things in your refrigeratior(countitems-복수형)
ex. bananas, eggs, bread, …

1. _____
2. _____
3. _____
4. _____
5. _____
6. _____
7. _____
8. _____

Questions using How many and How much

- Many and much are used with count and non-count nouns.
- Many can only be used with count nouns.
- Much can only be used with non-count nouns.

 To ask about number:

How many books   are   there?   There are 3 books.

To ask about amount:

How much time   is   there?   There is a lot.

There is a little.

There isn't much.

To ask about price:

How much (money) is   the computer?   It is $2,000.

💬 Write is or are in the blank.

1. How much _____ a cup of coffee at your favorite cafe?

2. How much _____ the shirt you are wearing?

3. How much _____ movie tickets?

4. How much _____ it to order chicken?

5. How much _____ coloring books?

6. How much _____ glasses at the glasses store?

For extra practice and numbers in English, see appendix Page 82.

Count and Non-count

Write "NC" for non-count or "C" for count in the blanks next to each noun.

 My Best Dish

When I am really hungry, I like to make burritos _____ . I need a lot of ingredients _____ to make a good burrito. First I need tomatoes _____ , onions, cilantro _____ (고수), and salt _____ for the sauce. The main part of the burrito is made of beans and beef _____ . Put all of these ingredients in a tortilla _____ and eat it with chili. Some people add avocados _____ and cheese _____ to give the burrito more flavor. A good drink to match with a burrito is cold soda _____ . The burrito can be a bit salty, so soda balances the flavors _____ well.

Questions

1. What ingredients do you need for the sauce?

2. What ingredients do you need for the main part?

3. What extra ingredients can you add for flavor?

4. What is best to drink with a burrito?

Simple & Practical English for Korean Students: A Beginner's Course

Unit
10

Comparative/
Superlative
Adjectives

Adjectives + er, est

Comparative/
Superlative Adjectives
Adjectives + er, est

✏ Comparative Adjectives

These are used to compare 2 things.

- John is tall**er** than Paul.
- John is thinn**er** than Paul.
- John is _more_ handsome than Paul.
- John is _more_ intelligent than Paul.
- For short words, "er" is added.
- For long words, "more/less" is added.

- Paul is short**er** than John.
- Paul is fatt**er** than John.
- Paul is _less_ handsome than John.
- Paul is _less_ intelligent than John.

💬 Make the following sentences.

- Elephant/mouse/big _____.

- Sharks/dolphins/dangerous _____.

- Tortoise/rabbit/fast _____.

- Mt Halla/Mt Everest/high _____.

- Bear/Sheep/strong _____.

💬 It's important to remember not to double up when using comparatives.

💬 The word "more" is not needed because "taller" already means "more tall".

Ex. My father is more taller than my uncle.

💬 The "-er" on the word "sweet" is not needed because the word "less" has that meaning.

Ex. Beer is usually less sweeter than cola.

💬 These are used to describe 1 in a group.

- John is the tall<u>est</u> student.
- John is the <u>most</u> intelligent student.
- For short words, "est" is added.
- For long words, "most/least" is added.

- Paul is the short<u>est</u> student.
- Paul is the <u>least</u> intelligent student.

💬 There are a couple of exceptions:

Good → Better → Best
Bad → Worse → Worst
Many → More → Most

💬 Make the following sentences.

- Roses/popular flowers _____.

- Elephants/long nose _____.

- Mt Everest/high mountain _____.

- Russia/large country _____.

- China/many people _____.

💬 As with comparative adjectives, it's important to remember not to double up.

💬 The word "most" is not needed because the word "tallest" has that meaning.

Ex. I am the <u>most tallest</u> in my class.

💬 The "-est" is not needed because the word "least" has that meaning.

Ex. My friend is the <u>least tallest</u> in the class.

💬 Compare these rivals. Make 1 comparative sentence and 1 superlative sentence.

- Drinks   Cola and Orange Juice

  Comparative: _____.

  Superlative: _____.

- Comics   Comic books and webtoons

  Comparative: _____.

  Superlative: _____.

- Music   K-pop and Rock

  Comparative: _____.

  Superlative: _____.

- Seasons   Summer and Winter

  Comparative: _____.

  Superlative: _____.

- Food   BBQ pork and Chicken soup

  Comparative: _____.

  Superlative: _____.

- Phones   Galaxy and i-phone

  Comparative: _____.

  Superlative: _____.

Now make some sentences of your own using the items you and your partner have On your desks or in your bags.

Friends and Sports

My friend Anna and I like sports. My favorite sport is baseball and her favorite sport is basketball. She says basketball is ❶ _____ (fun) than baseball because it is ❷ _____ (active). She says basketball is ❸ _____ (exciting) than baseball and playing basketball is ❹ _____ (easy) than playing baseball. To her, basketball is the best sport. I disagree. I think baseball is ❺ _____ (interesting) than basketball. It is true that baseball is ❻ _____ (complex) than basketball, but that is why it is ❼ _____ (fun). The most skillful athletes play baseball because it is the greatest sport.

 Underline the two superlatives in the story.

Ex. She thinks it is <u>the most expensive</u>.

 Questions

1. What is Anna's favorite sport?

2. Which sport is more active?

3. Which sport is more complex?

4. What kind of athletes play baseball?

Simple & Practical English for Korean Students: A Beginner's Course

Compound Sentences

Using but, and, so, or to join sentences

Unit 11

Compound Sentences

Using but, and, so, or to join sentences

The general pattern is

sentence + conjunction + sentence

Conjunctions

and	but	or	so	because

e.g.

- She goes to the store <u>and</u> buys clothes for her brother. (added information)

- Mike wanted to go to the birthday party, <u>but</u> he was sick. (opposite information)

- We will go to Everland <u>or</u> we will stay home. (two choices)

- I was tired <u>so</u> I went to bed early. (continuing information)

- It's hot <u>because</u> it's the middle of August. (reason)

About you

- Why do you study English?

- Why are you happy today?

- In the theater, do you like to sit in the front or the back? Why?

- Do you like city life or country life? Why?

💬 Practice sentences by putting these sentences together using "and, but, or, so".

1. I like spicy food. I don't like Chonyang Peppers.

   _____.

2. Mary thinks this music is good. I agree with Mary.

   _____.

3. Does he like hot noodles? Does he like cold noodles?

   _____.

4. I'm very tired. I don't want to do my homework now.

   _____.

5. He got a job at an office. It was not good.

   _____.

6. I can go to Lotte World today. I can go to Everland.

   _____.

7. They want to go to the festival. They don't have any money.

   _____.

8. Let's go to the new Chinese restaurant. We can stay home and

   order chicken.

   _____.

💬 Read the story and circle the correct conjunction.

There was big news about a new restaurant opening in Gangnam. It is a fusion restaurant of Korean (and/but) Western food. I wanted to eat there on opening day (but/or) I couldn't because I work late. Finally, I went there (but/and) I had a choice of eating a rice dish (but/or) pasta. I chose mixed rice (and/or) it was delicious. The food was really good (and/but) it was a little expensive. Going once in a while is okay, (or/but) I wouldn't go there often because of the price.

💬 Finish the sentence using "and, but, or, so" and check sentences with your partner.

1. I like playing PC games⋯

2. I am smart⋯

3. I can practice English for a long time⋯

4. She can buy that bag⋯

5. He drinks coffee at the cafe⋯

6. We can eat pasta⋯

7. They exercise in the park⋯

✏️ **Using but & and to talk about pros and cons of your future job.**

💬 **Job:** I want to work as a ground crew at the airport.

💬 **Pros:** It is a nice job AND I can travel.

💬 **Pros and Cons:**

- I can travel, BUT I won't have a lot of free time.
- Think of the job you want. What are four pros and four cons about that job?

Pros	Cons
1.	1.
2.	2.
3.	3.
4.	4.

Practice using "because" to connect reasons and results. Answer the Questions

1. A: I am so happy today!.

   B: Why?

   A: I got a new job!

   _____.

2. A: I want to go home.

   B: Why?

   A: I don't feel very good.

   _____.

3. A: They didn't like him very much.

   B: Why not?

   A: He didn't have good manners.

   _____.

4. A: He is studying English.

   B: Why?

   A: He wants to communicate with other people.

   _____.

5. A: She wants to live in the countryside.

   B: Why?

   A: The city is too busy and noisy.

   _____.

6. A: She wants to sit in the back

   B: Why?

   A: It is cooler in the back.

   _____ .

Now change these sentences to use the word "so" instead of "because".

Compound sentences

Fill in the blanks with and/or/so/but

💬 An Awesome Movie

I saw a movie yesterday about a detective. The movie was exciting ❶ _____ it had a lot of action. The actors were all famous ❷ _____ some of them couldn't act well. The main character was great because he is handsome and can fight well. The end of the movie was great ❸ _____ it was fun to watch. I usually don't watch crime movies. I watch comedy movies ❹ _____ I watch sci-fi movies. This crime movie was good ❺ _____ I might watch more crime movies in the future.

1. What was the movie about?

2. What part of the movie was great?

3. What kind of movies does he want to watch in the future?

Appendix

✏️ **Common Contractions**

Contractions are two words that have been written together usually with one or more letters replaced by an apostrophe '.

For example,

$$I + am = I'm$$

Contractions are easy to see in English because they are used so often. Students often ask what the differences are between the two words and the contraction. The difference is only the level of formality 언어의 격식.

- **Formal:** I do not study Spanish. (used mostly for formal writing, not speaking)
- **Less formal:** I don't study Spanish.

💬 **Common contractions**

With "not" → Do not – Don't
Will not – Won't

With "will" → I will – I'll
You will – You'll
He will– He'll
She will – She'll
We wil l– We'll
They will – They'll

With "have" → I have – I've
You have – You've
He has* – He's
She has* – She's
It has* – It's
We have – We've
They have –
They've

With "be" → I am – I'm
You are – You're
He is – He's**
She is – She's**
It is – It's **
We are– We're
They are – They're

* has is used here because of 3rd person singular(3인칭 단수 대명사)

** These contractions are the same as "he has/she has/it has" the difference can be seen in the predicate(술부) of the sentence

✏️ Contraction Practice

- Contractions show up a lot in the exercises of this book.
- Below are pairs of words. There will be a theme for each section. Look at the word pairs and write a sentence using the contraction of the two words.

💬 About summer

1. I will _____ .

2. She will _____ .

3. We will not _____ .

4. They are _____ .

5. He does not _____ .

💬 About winter

1. He has _____ .

2. It is _____ .

3. We do not _____ .

4. I will not _____ .

5. You are _____ .

Using the present tense, write your daily routine.

💬 Daily Weekday Routine

____AM   1. I wake up.

2. _____ .

3. _____ .

____FM   4. _____ .

5. _____ .

6. _____ .

7. _____ .

After writing your daily routine, ask your partner questions about your routine.

Friend   What time do you eat breakfast?
You   I eat breakfast at 7am.
You   What do you think I eat for breakfast?
Friend   I think you eat ⋯

Is your friend right or wrong?

When using the present tense, it is possible to say how often you do an action. If you do any action a lot you can use the term "always" to explain the situation.

 I always go to the market.

If you do not do the action a lot, you can use "rarely" or if you don't do the action, you can "never" to explain the situation.

 I rarely go to Paju.
I never smoke.

There is a list to use for words that describe how often from "always" 100% to "never" 0%.

Always	100%
Often	
Sometimes	
Rarely	
Never	0%

Use this list to talk about actions that you do and how often you do them.

1. (Always) _____.

2. (Sometimes) _____.

3. (Rarely) _____.

4. (Never) _____.

Present Continuous is used to describe actions that are happening at the present moment.

 She is talking on the phone (right now).

The words "right now" are in the sentence, but this information is already in the grammar.

Read the story below and write our 4 sentences that Tom is doing right now:

Time: 11:00am – Tom went to the shopping mall. He had to buy some clothes and some items for school. He is also a little hungry. Maybe he will see a friend here because many live in the area.

Time: 11:30

Write 5 actions that Tom might be doing now in Present Continuous.

1. _____.

2. _____.

3. _____.

4. _____.

5. _____.

Unit 4 - Future tense

"Will/be going to" are used for things that you are sure of.

For things that are unsure, "want to/would like to" are used. Also "maybe/might" can be used.

 I'm not sure, I want to eat pizza tomorrow.
I would like to go to Japan for my vacation.

These are future wishes/plans, but things might change.

"Will" and "be going to" are both used to talk about the future. The difference is the nuance that "be going to" has.

> Be going to: showing that you are sure of a future action (because of intention or information)

- I am going to travel to Rome. (I already bought my ticket so I am sure)
- It is going to rain today. (I saw the weather forecast so I'm sure)
- I am going to go to school Monday to Friday. (it is on my schedule so I am sure)

Look at the situations and write a sentence using "be going to" if it is a sure thing or a sentence using "will" if you can't be sure.

Ex. I reserved a KTX ticket to Busan next week.
I am going to go to Busan next week.

1. I reserved a table at Benny's Restaurant.

   _____.

2. I saw tomorrow's rainy forecast on the news.

   _____.

3. I am thinking about going camping, but I have no plan.

   _____.

Unit 6 - Gerunds and Infinitives

Most of the time gerunds and infinitives have the same or similar meaning:

 e.g. I like eating pizza. = I like to eat pizza.

However, there are some situations in which the gerund sentence has a different meaning compared to the infinitive sentence:

 Example 1

- Talking about past (using gerund)
- I will always remember driving to school.

- Talking about future (using infinitive)
- Remember to drive safe tomorrow!

Example 2

- Talking about past
- She forgets spending money on Lotto tickets.

- Talking about the future
- Don't forget to spend the leftover money.

 Practice

Read the situation and write what the person will say following the examples above.

1. Your brother is telling you to wear warm clothes tomorrow:

   Remember _____ .

2. Your mother is talking about how you always forget your keys:

   Don't forget _____ .

3. Your friend is reminding you of a time you ate all of the pizza:

Remember _____.

💬 My Dog Doongi

My name is Jeff. I will tell you about my dog. His name is Doon-gi and he loves ❶ _____(play). I remember ❷ _____(take) him to the park and I remember ❸ _____(play) for hours. He enjoys ❹ _____(run) in the snow in Winter and ❺ _____ (swim) in the Summer. I tried ❻ _____(train) him, but he doesn't like ❼ _____(follow) my words. He also dislikes ❽ _____(go) to the animal hospital. Even though he doesn't follow me, I want ❾ _____(be) with him forever.

🔍 Questions

1. What does Doongi love doing?

_____.

2. What does Doongi enjoy doing in the Winter?

_____.

3. What does Doongi dislike doing?

_____.

4. What does Jeff want?

_____.

Look at the picture and write the location of the objects.

1. Where are the pens?

   _____.

2. Where is the stuffed animal?

   _____.

3. Where is the calendar(달력)?

   _____.

4. Where is the coffee cup?

   _____.

Rules are for things that you have no choice in. Advice is just a good idea that you can choose to follow.

Rules	Advice
Positive form	**Positive form**
· You <u>must</u> have a license to drive a car.	· You <u>should</u> exercise every day.
· You <u>have to</u> be on time to class.	· You <u>can</u> drink water in class.
· You <u>need to</u> bring your bus/subway card.	
Negative form	**Negative form**
· You <u>must not</u> smoke in the class-room.	· You <u>shouldn't</u> smoke.
· You <u>can't</u> use your phone in the movie theater.	· You <u>don't have to</u> wear a jacket.
	· You <u>don't need to</u> always ride the bus.

- When using "have to/need to" there is no choice.
- When using "don't have to/don't need to" there is a choice.

- When using "can't" there is no choice.
- When using "can" there is a choice.

- "Should/shouldn't" are for ideas that are thought to be good in some way.
- "Can/don't need to/don't have to" have no feeling, good or bad, attached to them.

Practice the nuance (미묘한 차이)

1. The students _____ be on time to class.

2. I _____ go to school on Tuesdays.

3. I _____ wear a uniform to class.

4. People who work in Korea _____ pay tax.

5. We _____ drive to school, we can take the bus.

6. A doctor _____ have a university degree.

7. Taxi drivers _____ know how to drive a bus.

8. A police officer _____ be a man.

9. A doctor _____ smoke cigarettes.

10. We _____ fight in the classroom.

11. A chef _____ be careful in the kitchen.

12. A accountant _____ exercise every day.

Number chart in English

	thousand	Million	Billion	Trillion
1	000	000	000	000
10	000	000	000	000
100	000	000	000	000

 e.g. 100,000,002 = one million and two

100,004 = one hundred thousand and four

1. 11,473 = _____ .

2. 923,872 = _____ .

3. 137,907,001 = _____ .

4. 10,475,205 = _____ .

5. 1,496 = _____ .

6. Fifteen thousand and eleven = _____ .

7. Eight hundred and forty-three thousand = _____ .

8. One thousand six hundred and six = _____ .

9. Six trillion eight hundred seventy three thousand = _____ .

10. Twenty two million two hundred forty four thousand = _____ .

💬 Write much or many in the blank.

1. a. How _____ is a book?

   b. ₩15,000.

2. a. How _____ Web-toons do you follow?

   b. 7 at the moment.

3. a. How _____ are the Gundam Models?

   b. W70,000 for each model.

4. a. How _____ cellphones does he have?

   b. He has 2 cellphones.

5. a. How _____ is it online?

   b. It is only W25,000!

6. a. How _____ movies have you seen this month?

   b. 3 so far.

7. a. How _____ is it at the store?

   b. It is 5,000 won cheaper than online.

Comparatives are used to show what is more or less than something else.

 The zoo is <u>more exciting than</u> the museum.

Superlatives are used to show what is the most or least of all things.

 The amusement park is <u>the most exciting</u>.

To explain how two things are equal or on the same level, use "as adjective as".

 The amusement park is <u>as exciting as</u> the singing rooms (노래방).

Use these adjective to describe things that are equal.

1. (Boring) _____.

2. (Interesting) _____.

3. (Delicious) _____.

4. (Easy) _____.

5. (Dynamic) _____.

Answer Key

💬 Unit 1

• P. 10

1. <u>What is</u> your name?

2. <u>Is</u> your teacher from Canada?

3. <u>Where are</u> you from?

4. <u>What do</u> you do after school?

5. <u>When is</u> your birthday?

6. <u>Are</u> they from Australia?

7. <u>What is</u> their favorite sport?

8. <u>What does</u> your friend do in the weekends?

9. <u>Do</u> you like your school?

10. <u>What do</u> you do in your free time?

Fill in the blanks: is, sketches, goes, finds, says, is, puts, draws, likes, gives, are

• P. 11

1. What's her hobby? - Her hobby is sketching. Her hobby is art.

2. Where does she like to go? - She likes to go to the park.

3. What does she try to find? - She tries to find interesting things to sketch.

4. Who likes her drawings? - Her friend really likes her drawings, as well as other people.

5. Where can people see her drawings? - People can see her drawings in cafes or offices.

6. What does she say is the best thing to sketch? - She says people doing something together is the best thing to sketch.

7. Why does she think so? - Because she puts feeling into the drawing.

Unit 2

• P. 17

My name <u>is</u> Jenny. My friend, Kim, <u>is</u> in my class at school. We <u>are</u> both students. We <u>are</u> different in many ways. I <u>have</u> 3 brothers but Kim <u>doesn't have</u> any brothers or sisters. I <u>live</u> with my parents but Kim <u>lives</u> alone. At university I <u>study</u> design and Kim <u>studies</u> science. Kim <u>doesn't work</u>, but I <u>work</u> at a restaurant. I <u>like</u> rock music, but Kim <u>doesn't like</u> it. She <u>watches</u> YouTube videos. We usually <u>watch</u> movies together on Saturdays.

1. Where does jenny work? - She works in a restaurant.

2. What is Kim's hobby? - Kim watches YouTube videos.

3. Who lives alone? - Kim lives alone.

4. Is Jenny an only child? - No she isn't. She has 3 brothers.

5. What does Kim study? - Kim studies science.

6. What do they usually do on Saturdays? - They usually watch movies together.

• P. 19

1. Her brother doesn't study every day.

2. They study at night.

3. I go to Busan in the summer.

Unit 3

• P. 23

1. is buying

2. are eating

3. is riding

4. isn't studying/is playing

5. aren't playing/are studying

6. are doing

7. am walking/isn't raining

8. are drinking

9. am relaxing/am reading

10. are ordering

• P. 24

1. What are you buying?

2. Where are you going?

3. When is the restaurant closing?/What time is the restaurant closing?

4. When is the movie starting?/What time is the movie starting?

5. What are they listening to?

6. How are they going there?

• P. 25

Mark	Hey Ron!
Ron	Oh, hi Mark!
Mark	What are you doing right now?
Ron	I'm ❶ watching cat videos on youtube. They're so funny.
Mark	Ha! I'm ❷ playing with my cat now. Maybe I can make a video.
Ron	Want to do something? I am bored. I'm just sitting around watching videos.
Mark	Yea, I'm not ❸ doing anything.
Ron	Let's meet at Sadang Station.
Mark	Ok, but how will I find you? What are you wearing?
Ron	I'm ❹ wearing a black hat and white sweater. You?
Mark	I'm ❺ wearing my new long padded jacket. You'll know when you see it.
Ron	Cool! See you soon.

1. Ron is watching cat videos on Youtube.

2. Mark is playing with his cat.

3. Ron is wearing a black hat and a white sweater.

4. Mark is wearing his new long padded jacket.

• P. 27

1. I am running now.

2. They are meeting in front of Anyang station.

3. 3. I am always watching YouTube videos.

Unit 4

• P. 31

1. will
2. will not/ won't
3. will
4. will not/ won't
5. will

1. am going to
2. are not go- ing to
3. is going to
4. is going to
5. are going to

• P. 35

1. Luna is going to go to Malaysia.

2. His friend is going to buy a new car.

3. I am going to eat pizza for dinner tonight.

Unit 5

• P. 40

Last Summer, I <u>went</u> to Busan. I <u>took</u> the fast train to Busan Station.

It <u>was</u> so fast! I <u>went</u> to Haeundae Beach first.

I <u>swam</u> in the water and <u>drank</u> some soda while relaxing. It <u>was</u> so nice.

Later, I <u>went</u> to the night market and <u>bought</u> some street food.

The night market <u>had</u> a good atmosphere. I also <u>tried</u> really delicious seafood.

After, I <u>went</u> to Gwangali Beach and <u>took</u> pictures next to the water.

The ocean wind <u>felt</u> really nice. I want to go to Busan again.

• P. 41

1. ate
2. saw
3. texted
4. had
5. stayed up
6. spent
7. drank

1. Did you eat BBQ with friends last week?

2. Did you see the new drama on MBC yesterday?

3. Did you text your friend to see what was happening?

4. Did you have breakfast this morning?

5. Did you stay up late playing games on your phone last night?

6. Did you spend all of your money on payday?

7. Did you drink a lot of water last summer?

• P. 44

1. Present: Dr Lee <u>gets up</u> early in the morning for his class.

   Present Continuous: Dr Lee <u>is getting up</u> early in the morning for his class.

   Future _(going to): Dr Lee <u>is going to get up</u> early in the morning for his class.

   Past: Dr Lee <u>got up</u> early in the morning for his class.

2. Present: My friend <u>brings</u> a cake to the class and we <u>eat</u> it with everybody.

   Present Continuous: My friend <u>is bringing</u> a cake to the class and we <u>are eating</u> it with everybody.

   Future _(will): My friend <u>will bring</u> a cake to the class and we <u>will eat</u> it with everybody.

   Past: My friend <u>brought</u> a cake to the class and we <u>ate</u> it with everybody.

3. Present: My dad <u>goes</u> to Canada during the winter and <u>catches</u> a cold there.

   Present Continuous: My dad <u>is going</u> to Canada during the winter and <u>is catching</u> a cold there.

   Future _(going to): My dad <u>is going to go</u> to Canada during the winter and <u>is going to catch</u> a cold there.

   Past: My dad <u>went</u> to Canada during the winter and <u>caught</u> a cold there.

4. Present: I <u>travel</u> to New York city because my family lives there.

   Present Continuous: I <u>am travelling</u> to New York city because my family lives there.

   Future _(will): I <u>will travel</u> to New York city because my family lives there.

   Past: I <u>travelled</u> to New York city because my family lives there.

5. Present: They <u>play</u> basketball on Saturday in a team.

   Present Continuous: They <u>are playing</u> basketball on Saturday in a team.

   Future _(going to): They <u>are going to</u> play basketball on Saturday in a team.

   Past: They <u>played</u> basketball on Saturday in a team.

6. Present: She <u>meets</u> him on the airplane to Japan and <u>falls</u> in love with him.

   Present Continuous: She <u>is meeting</u> him on the airplane to Japan and <u>is falling</u> in love with him.

   Future _(will): She <u>will meet</u> him on the airplane to Japan and <u>will fall</u> in love with him.

   Past: She <u>met</u> him on the airplane to Japan and <u>fell</u> in love with him.

7. Present: Chris <u>gives</u> his girlfriend a nice birthday present. So she <u>pays</u> for dinner.

   Present Continuous: Chris <u>is giving</u> his girlfriend a nice birthday present. So she <u>is paying</u> for dinner.

Future (going to): Chris <u>will give</u> his girlfriend a nice birthday present. So she <u>will pay</u> for dinner.

Past: Chris <u>gave</u> his girlfriend a nice birthday present. So she <u>paid</u> for dinner.

8. Present: I <u>find</u> someone's wallet on the street. I <u>take</u> it to the police station.

Present Continuous: I <u>am finding</u> someone's wallet on the street. I <u>am taking</u> it to the police station.

Future (will): I <u>will find</u> someone's wallet on the street. I <u>will take</u> it to the police station.

Past: I <u>found</u> someone's wallet on the street. I <u>took</u> it to the police station.

9. Present: My mother <u>comes</u> home really late from work.

Present Continuous: My mother <u>is coming</u> home really late from work.

Future (going to): My mother <u>is going to come</u> home really late from work.

Past: My mother <u>came</u> home really late from work.

 Unit 6

• P. 53

1. I want to go home.

2. I like taking a trip to Busan.

3. I enjoy watching videos online.

 Unit 7

• P. 57

I am always in my room. I don't clean it often, but I know where everything is. I will tell you where my most important items are. I have a nice gaming PC ❶ <u>next to</u> my bed. I play games there every night with friends. I have a heating mat ❷ <u>on</u> my bed to keep me warm on cold nights. I have a projector so I can watch movies of the ceiling ❸ <u>above</u> my bed. I have a pet turtle ❹ <u>in</u> a glass case. His name is Bitey. He is always ❺ <u>under</u> the water. I always have my guitar ❻ <u>between</u> my bed and my desk. I play it sometimes. I love my room!

1. Fredrick's gaming PC is next to his bed.

2. Fredrick's heating mat is on his bed.

   Bitey is in his glass case/under the water.

3. Fredrick's guitar is between his bed and his desk.

• P. 61

1. Go straight and turn left.

2. Turn left and pass the bank.

3. I'm standing next to the building.

💬 Unit 9

• P. 71

Countable foods: Banana, Tomato, Egg, Apple, Potato, Onion

Non-count foods: Milk, Toast, Oil, Chicken, Pork, Bacon, Ramen, Pepper paste, Rice, Kimchi, Coffee, Butter

• P. 73

1. Uncountable	2. Countable	3. Uncountable
4. Countable	5. Uncountable	6. Uncountable
7. Uncountable	8. Countable	9. Countable
10. Uncountable		

• P. 74

1. some	2. some	3. a	4. some	5. a
6. some	7. some	8. an	9. a	10. an

• P. 76

1. is	2. is	3. are	4. is	5. are	6. are

• P. 77

My Best Dish

When I am really hungry, I like to make burritos ___C___ . I need a lot of ingredients ___NC___ to make a good burrito. First I need tomatoes ___C___ , onions, cilantro ___NC___ (고수), and salt ___NC___ for the sauce. The main part of the burrito is made of beans and beef ___NC___ . Put all of these ingredients in a tortilla
___C___ and eat it with chili. Some people add avocados ___C___ and cheese
___NC___ to give the burrito more flavor. A good drink to match with a burrito
is cold soda ___NC___ . The burrito can be a bit salty, so soda balances the flavors ___C___ well.

1. You need tomatoes, onions, cilantro, and salt.

2. You need beans and beef.

3. You can add avocados and cheese.

4. Soda is best to drink with a burrito.

Unit 10

• P. 81

An elephant is bigger than a mouse
Sharks are more dangerous than dolphins
A rabbit is faster than a tortoise
Mt Everest is higher than Mt Halla
A bear is stronger than a sheep

• P. 83

Roses are the most popular flowers
Elephants have the longest nose
Mt Everest is the highest mountain
Russia is the largest country
China has the most people

• P. 85

Friends and Sports

My friend Anna and I like sports. My favorite sport is baseball and her favorite sport is basketball. She says basketball is ❶ <u>more fun</u> than baseball because it is ❷ <u>more active</u>. She says basketball is ❸ <u>more exciting</u> than baseball and playing basketball is ❹ <u>easier</u> than playing baseball. To her, basketball is <u>the best sport</u>. I disagree. I think baseball is ❺ <u>more interesting</u> than basketball. It is true that baseball is ❻ <u>more complex</u> than basketball, but that is why it is ❼ <u>more fun</u>. The most skillful athletes play baseball because it is <u>the greatest sport</u>.

1. Anna's favorite sport is basketball.

2. Basketball is more active (than baseball).

3. Baseball is more complex (than basketball).

4. The most skilled athletes play baseball.

💬 Unit 11

• P. 89

1. but   2. and   3. or   4. so   5. but   6. or   7. but   8. or

and, but, and, or, and, but, but

• P. 93

An Awesome Movie

I saw a movie yesterday about a detective. The movie was exciting ❶ <u>and</u> it had a lot of action. The actors were all famous ❷ <u>but</u> some of them couldn't act well. The main character was great because he is handsome and can fight well. The end of the movie was great ❸ <u>so</u> it was fun to watch. I usually don't watch crime movies. I watch comedy movies ❹ <u>or</u> I watch sci-fi movies. This crime movie was good ❺ <u>so</u> I might watch more crime movies in the future.

1. The movie was about a detective.

2. The end of the movie was great.

3. He wants to watch more crime movies in the future.

💬 Appendix

• P. 100

1. Remember to wear warm clothes tomorrow.

2. Don't forget to take your keys.

3. Remember eating all the pizza?

• P. 102

1. The pens are in the pen can.

2. The stuffed animal is under the monitor.

3. The calendar is between the monitor and the pen can.

4. The coffee cup is next to the pen can.

• P. 104

1. must/have to/need to	2. should
3. have to/don't have to	4. must/have to
5. don't have to/don't need to	6. must/has to/needs to
7. don't have to/don't need to	8. doesn't have to/doesn't need to
9. can/shouldn't	10. must not/can't
11. must/has to/needs to/should	12. doesn't have to/doesn't need to/should

• P. 105

1. eleven thousand four hundred and seventy-three

2. nine hundred and twenty-three thousand eight hundred and seventy two

3. one hundred and thirty seven million nine hundred and seven thousand and one

4. ten million four hundred and seventy-five thousand two hundred and five

5. one thousand four hundred and ninety-six

6. 15,011

7. 843,000

8. 1,606

9. 6,000,000,873,000

10. 22,244,000

• P. 106

1. much	2. many	3. much	4. many
5. much	6. many	7. much	

Simple & Practical
English for
Korean Students:A
Beginner's Course

Commonly Difficult Vowel Sounds

Vowels (모음) are open sounds between consonants (자음). The sounds for a vowel can be explained by tongue placement (혀 위치), and below, they will be described by front- back and high-low tongue placement.

Native Korean speakers often have difficulty with the following vowel sounds (모음인 음) when learning Standard American English:

Tongue Placement(혀의 위치)	Letters	Example
· Back end vowel, high · Back end vowel, low	· ee · i	· Feel (higher pitch farther back) · The wind feels good. · Fill (more relaxed back center) · I fill the glass with water.
· Central vowel +_r, high · Front- end vowel + l, low	· or · al	· Work (central vowel high) · I work at home. · Walk (front end vowel- low- open mouth*) · I walk home. * many speakers can improve by opening their mouth wider when pronouncing "al" sounds
· Front-end vowel, low	· o	· so* · I am hungry so I'll buy a sandwich. * This "o" sound is less rounded that the Korean "오" · If saying "소" there is more rounding of the lips than the "so" in American English.

Even with incorrect pronunciation, most of these words can be understood.

Pronunciation Practice for Vowels

Below will be a word that is commonly mispronounced. Make a sentence with that word and practice saying the sentence aloud using proper tongue placement.

About travel:

Feel _____.

Fill _____.

So _____.

Work _____.

Walk _____.

Note: The vowels covered here are not the only mistakes students make, but are the most common mistakes students make while using this book to study.

Commonly Difficult Consonant Sounds

Consonants (자음) are the sounds that can be at the front or end of vowels (모음). The sounds for the consonants below can be explained using different parts of the mouth: the teeth (치음), the lips and teeth (순치음), area behind teeth (치경음), and more. However, we will focus on these three areas for this practice.

Parts of the Mouth(조음기관)	Letters	Examples
• Area behind teeth(치경음)	• R • L	• Fear (tongue doesn't touch the top of the mouth) • I don't fear the dark. • Feel (Tongue touches the top of the mouth) • I don't feel warm in winter.
• Between teeth(치음)	• TH	• This (voice is used) • This is good. • Thank you (voice is not used). • Thank you for helping me.
• Lips and teeth(순치음)	• V • F	• Very (voice is used) • The food is very good. • Ferry (voice is not used) • Take the ferry from Busan to Hakata.

Pronunciation Practice for Consonants

Below will be a word that is commonly mispronounced. Make a sentence with that word and practice saying the sentence aloud using proper parts of the mouth.

About School:

Very _____ .

Ferry _____ .

This _____ .

Thank you for _____ .

Fear _____ .

Feel _____ .

Note: The consonants covered here are not the only mistakes students make, but are the most common mistakes students make while using this book to study.

Blended Words

Blending is when groups of words are put together when spoken.

For example   I want to go to the beach → I wanna go to the beach.
This only happens in speaking and sometimes in text messages. This is because both can be used in informal (언어의 약식) situations. Below are common blended phrases in American English.

Common blended phrases

Want to - wanna

- I want to eat pizza.
- I wanna eat pizza.*
  *Useful for infinitives in Unit 6

Do you - dyuh

- Do you go to the park?
- Dyuh go to the park?**
  ** Useful for Yes/No questions in unit 1 & 2

What is your - whatcher

- What is your name?
- Whatcher name?***
  *** Useful for WH questions in Unit 2

And - en (n)

- I'll buy some apples and butter.
- I'll buy some apples en butter.
  or
  I'll buy some apples n butter.

What do you - whaddaya

- What do you like to play on PC -
- Whaddaya like to play on PC?
  ""Useful for Gerunds in Unit 6

Make a question

All of these blended sounds show up in the units of this book. After writing out the sentences, practice speaking them aloud to work on blending the sounds.

1. What is your _____.

2. English and Korean _____.

3. Do you _____.

4. What do you _____.

5. Do you want to _____.

Answer the question. Are there any blended words in the answers?

1. _____.

2. _____.

3. _____.

4. _____.

5. _____.

About the authors

Nicolas E. Caballero

- Bachelors of Arts (Philosophy)
  California State Polytechnic University, Pomona

- Masters of Arts (English)
  California State Polytechnic University, Pomona

- Over 10 years of teaching ESL and EFL abroad

Vaughan Taylor

- Bachelor of Commerce (Economics)
  University of Otago, New Zealand

- Master of Education (TESOL)
  University of Tasmania, Australia

- Over 20 years of teaching ESL in South Korea

Simple &
Practical English
for Korean Students:
A Beginner's Course

초판 1쇄 발행 2023년 2월 20일

저 자	Nicolas E. Caballero · Vaughan Taylor
펴낸이	임 순 재
펴낸곳	(주)한올출판사
등 록	제11-403호
주 소	서울시 마포구 모래내로 83(성산동 한올빌딩 3층)
전 화	(02) 376-4298(대표)
팩 스	(02) 302-8073
홈페이지	www.hanol.co.kr
e-메일	hanol@hanol.co.kr
ISBN	979-11-6647-320-3

Simple & Practical
English for
Korean Students:A
Beginner's Course

Simple & Practical
English for
Korean Students:A
Beginner's Course

Simple & Practical
English for
Korean Students:A
Beginner's Course